Deltek
Vantagepoint

Beyond Best Practices

First Edition

by
Tami Gentry

Kismet Publications Inc.
Buckeye, AZ

Published 2025

Deltek
Vantagepoint

Beyond Best Practices

Published by Kismet Publications Inc.
23260 North Sundance Parkway Suite 1226
Buckeye, AZ 85326
United States of America

Deltek Vantagepoint, Beyond Best
Practices was first published in 2025.

ISBN: 979-8-9932362-1-6
First Edition

Dedication

To Mom and Dad. Love you....

To the hard-working individuals who show up every day, and to the firms who take the risk to safeguard this country's infrastructure,

"Thank you."

Whether you use Vantagepoint for projects, operations, CRM, or accounting, this resource is here to help get you back to it by zooming out to give you a Bird's Eye View.

Table of Contents

Introduction

- The Speed of Business
- Migration Begins
- Holistic Costs

Chapter 1: What is an ERP?

- **Enterprise Resource Planning**

Chapter 2: Target Acquired

- Moving Target
- Red Flag City
- Bullseye

Chapter 3: Reaping the Rewards

- Strategic Alignment
- Process Improvement
- Comms, Training & Support

Solutions

- Pre-migration
- Mid-migration
- Post-migration

Introduction

The Speed of Business

Project lifecycles are not static. Invoices recur and payroll is always due. In a perfect world, contracts begin, contracts end and contracts begin again. Take your foot off the accelerator for a moment and the wheel may grind to a halt.

"How do we replace vital equipment while moving at the speed of business?"

Hire an Expert

Deltek Pros are the best in the business-professionals who do this sort of thing for a living. The software manufacturer trusts them to move your data and provide training for you. They know best practices and they're paid to tell you[r competitors].

Migration Begins

The decision has been made; the experts procured. Your firm is on the move. *Congratulations!*

Introduction

The Heavy Lifting

Vantagepoint is the choice. Project team members and system integrators are known. Licensing has been approved.

Executives are done, right?

Pick a date and wait, wait, wait!

...Right?!

Holistic Costs

Project costs are capped at the final amount shown at the bottom of the invoice, right?

...Right?!

Spoiler alert: there's going to be homework.

Chapter 1

 **What is an ERP?**

Enterprise Resource Planning

Once upon a time, folks had individual files, and folders were personal.

We spent a lot of time sharing our files and data...

...with other folks and other departments.

Enterprise Resource Planning

Fast forward to the age of computers.

In many cases...

...not much has changed.

Mergers, acquisitions and strategic growth often lead to the need for group efforts in operations and accounting.

ABC
Engineering
1960

ABC Engineering, Survey, Land Development, Construction Management, Accounting & Corporate 2024

ABC Inc.
2025 and
beyond

When this occurs, data analysis needs change.

Enterprise Resource Planning

Enter Enterprise Resource Planning (ERP) programs...

ERPs centralize apps used by the entire organization to facilitate workflows between departments and ease data analytic headaches.

Winning a contract begins with business development. Resources get hired and perform work. Accounting bills work, receives payment, and pays workers.

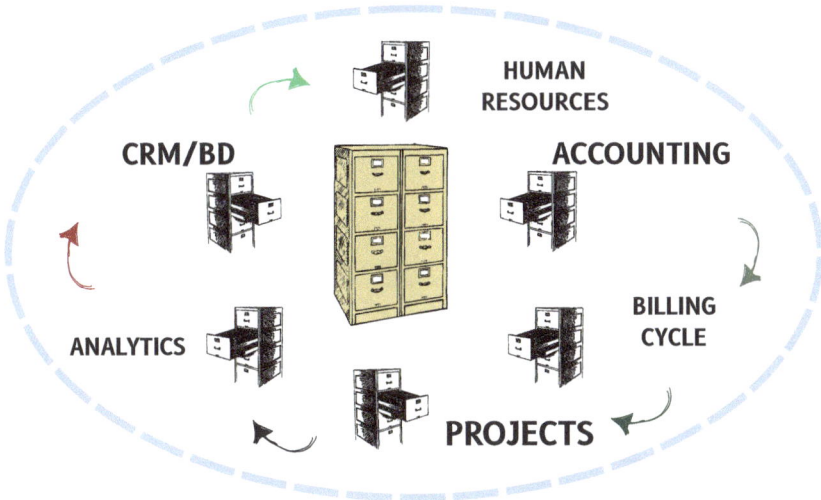

CRM/BD

HUMAN RESOURCES

ACCOUNTING

ANALYTICS

BILLING CYCLE

PROJECTS

These apps work together to store, share, calculate and more.

Chapter 2

Target Acquired

Beyond Best Practices

Project Lifecycle

"Our basic business model won't change when we upgrade. We will still pursue work, win contracts, execute project tasks, bill clients, get paid, pay resources, and analyze what we did. The new system was designed to support that, yes?"

Yes! The series of questions your Deltek assigned system integrator will ask are designed to extrapolate the settings needed to configure your copy of the new software according to your firm's unique service requirements, policies and procedures. Many firms take this opportunity to review what not working now (paper processes, the use of multiple systems to perform one task, lack of communication between departments) and consider where they'd like to be as a company (culture) in 5 or more years.

As time speeds on, and executives are slammed with the rigors of running a business, all too often the response from teams who haven't done their homework is, "What is best practice?"

"Best" practice is in the eye of the beholder.

Red Flag City

Anything But Homework

Migration is more than an upgrade. Reimagining how software stores your project files isn't always intuitive. Team dynamics may change in unanticipated ways. If the new normal isn't properly defined, it can lead firms into trouble.

Change of Perspective

Just as moving from physical files (with locked cabinets and locked doors) to cloud systems accessible by many prompted a change in thinking for the human culture, a change in business systems across multiple departments at once will entail much more than a copy and paste of the old system and a bit of automation. Your entire company culture may shift.

Organization Design Takes Time

When people are uncertain where the career path they've been working toward for 5-40 years is heading, shift can happen. Minimizing holistic costs is critical to gaining competitive advantage through project success. While firms can fall back on OD to implement significant change, relying on assigned system integrators to advise "best practice" is a recipe for disaster.

Moving Target

With the best of intentions, many project teams are aiming at a moving target...

...they aren't able to clearly see.

Zooming along the roadmap toward transition without a *Bird's Eye View* can feel like a daunting and murky prospect with an unclear end. Many teams put off their migration until they're forced to take the shot.

VVllp is here to assist internal teams with migration heavy lifting, dashboard development...

...and clean-up after the fact.

Vantagepoint Security Settings
Additional Training for PMs
Project Planning Tutorials

Moving Target

With the best of intentions, many project teams are aiming at a moving target...

...they aren't able to clearly see.

Zooming along the roadmap toward transition without a *Bird's Eye View* can feel like a daunting and murky prospect with an unclear end. Many teams put off their migration until they're forced to take the shot.

If you had to run a marathon tomorrow, could you estimate what your time would be? Great! Now add 300-5000 of your favorite coworkers and calculate that again. Take a little longer than if you were by yourself? ERP migrations are a little like that. To move as a unit requires direction, leadership, effort, and communication.

Training is *not* a bonus and **go-live** is *not* the end. It's the *beginning*.

Bullseye

Project Team

How will *you* hit a bullseye
from multiple perspectives?

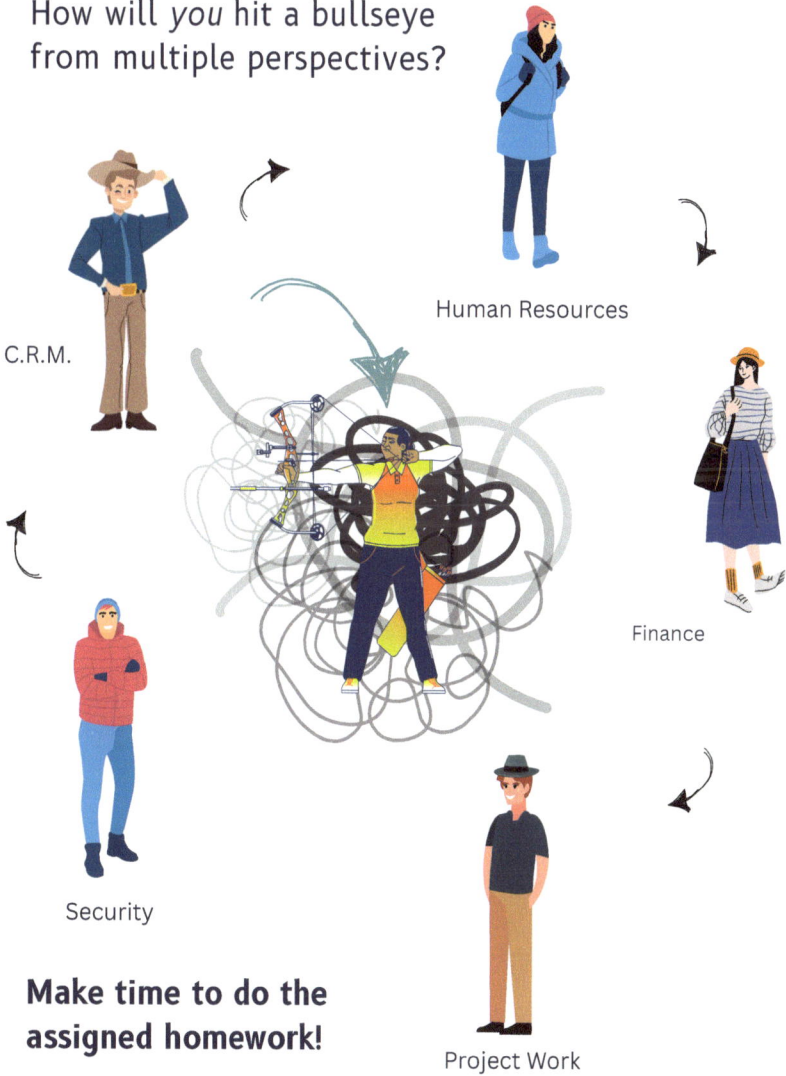

C.R.M.

Human Resources

Finance

Security

**Make time to do the
assigned homework!**

Project Work

Chapter 3

Reaping the Rewards

Strategic Alignment

Get Your Ship Together

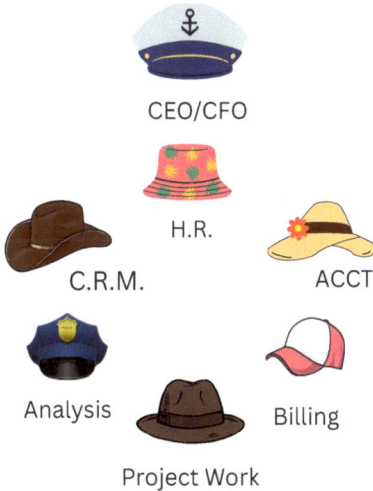

CEO/CFO

H.R.

C.R.M.

ACCT

Analysis

Billing

Project Work

A shared vision centralizes strategy to support staff whose skills are the secret sauce which create a differential between your firm and the competition.*

Resistance to change is a human reaction to a] fear of the unknown, b] loss and c] the recollection of past experiences. When structure, culture and technology change in an instant-for the *entire* company-efforts to communicate "the plan" early and often while remaining transparent about future uncertainty can lead to panic.

Complexity Gives A False Sense of Control

Just as the company's founders sat down and plotted what they wanted the company to be as it grew, so now you have the opportunity to do the same. Start over. Keep it simple. And remember, my brilliant engineering friends, we are programming *soft*ware, not constructing an obstacle course. Requests to rebuild complexities may be a signal of executives' unrecognized bias to change.

*McKinsey 7S Model (Waterman & Peters, 1980)

Process Improvement

Where do we plan to be in 5-10-15 years? ...And how do we get there from here?

Current State:
Work-arounds & fixes considered sole solution

- Revenue Methods
- Overhead Allocation
- Job Cost Adj.
- Rate Tables
- Billing Terms

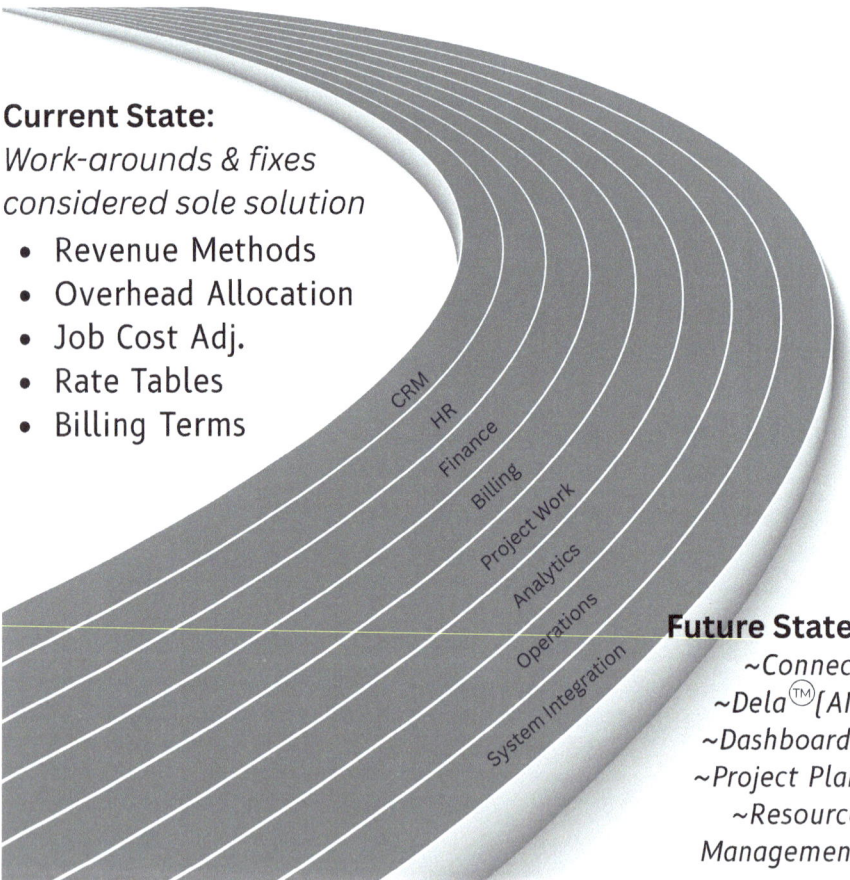

CRM
HR
Finance
Billing
Project Work
Analytics
Operations
System Integration

Future State:
~Connect
~Dela™ [AI]
~Dashboards
~Project Plan
~Resource Management

Communications

Break through the noise.

People are notification weary. We have hundreds of accounts and just as many items on the "to do" list as the "honey do" list. Tell me the essentials 10 times.

Training

Train often and on-demand.

Minds wander at the best of times. Most PMs have 37 project plates in the air and don't want to drop any. Training is needed in small bites, on-demand and played at their speed.

Solutions

<VV_llp>

<ERP SMEs>

Master
Certification

Resource Planning
Certification

Accounting
Certification

CRM
Certification

Advocate for You

Solutions

[VV llp]

Deltek Vantagepoint Customization & Training Consultants + System Admin. As A Service

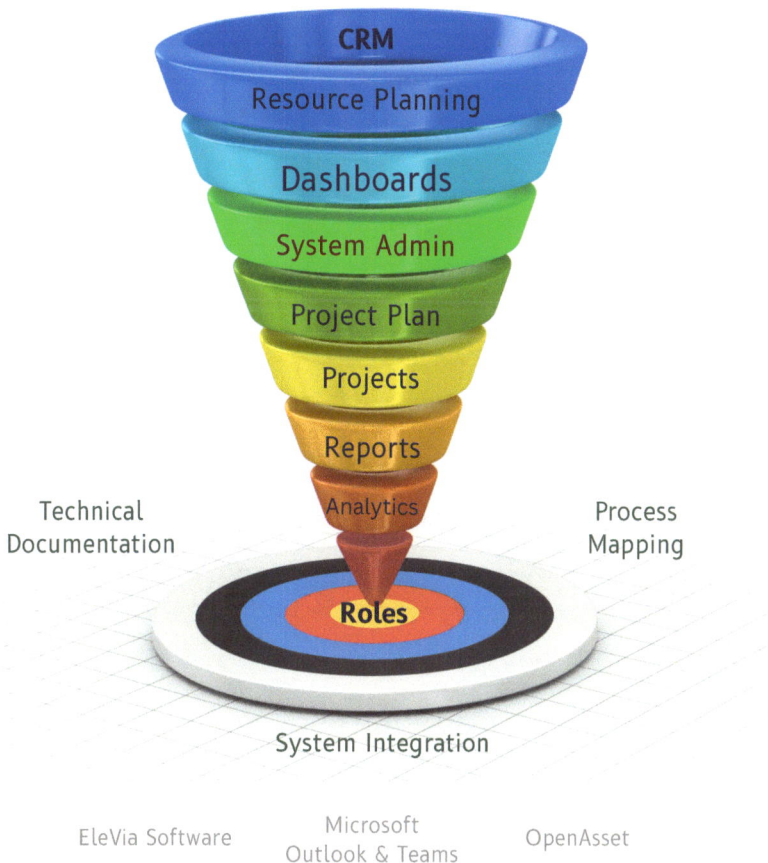

CRM

Resource Planning

Dashboards

System Admin

Project Plan

Projects

Reports

Analytics

Technical Documentation

Process Mapping

Roles

System Integration

EleVia Software

Microsoft Outlook & Teams

OpenAsset

Solutions

Pre-Migration

- Organization Design Support
  - Elicit Requirements
  - Document Current Processes, Proposed Processes, Decisions Made and Changes Anticipated, Make Recommendations
- System Configuration
  - System Security & Role Design
  - Screen Design Vp Preview(s) & Production
  - Troubleshoot Workflows, Custom Reports and Saved Searches
- Team Training or Refresher Training
- Business Transformation Advocacy

Post-Migration Evaluation

- Get Answers to Lingering Questions
- Request Improvement Roadmap
- Broken Workflows or Custom Reports

Post-Migration Support

- System Administration as a Service/Hr.
- On-going Initiative Roll-outs
  - Redesign Screens or Custom HUBs
  - Training by Role
  - Dashboards, Mobile CRM, Connect
  - Preparation for Best of Breed Integrations

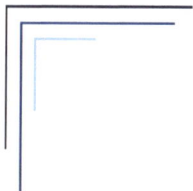

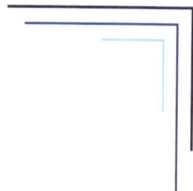

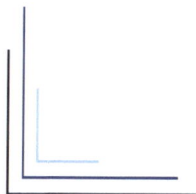

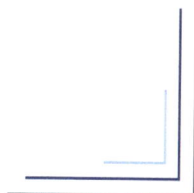

www.ingramcontent.com/pod-product-compliance
Lightning Source LLC
Chambersburg PA
CBHW041304290326
41931CB00032B/38